IT'S ABOUT
PEOPLE

D1609135

ROGER CAMPBELL

outskirts
press

Outskirts Press, Inc.
http://www.outskirtspress.com

ISBN: 978-1-4787-9993-1

Outskirts Press and the "OP" logo are trademarks belonging to Outskirts Press, Inc.

PRINTED IN THE UNITED STATES OF AMERICA

Table of Contents

Testimonials

It's About People by Roger Campbell is full of great time-proven examples of good leadership basics. This is a must-read for any in leadership that are just beginning the journey or for more senior leaders that are trying to get their business back on track.

I have had the pleasure of knowing and working with Roger for over twenty-five years, many as part of the Training Group at Worthington Industries.

I consider Roger to be my mentor, and I learned all the lessons he has written about here by observing him "in action" all those years. He personally practices everything he teaches in this book.

The lesson I most value is learning how everything in business—and in life itself—comes back to relationships. Roger has been a role model to me, and to countless others, for building and maintaining relationships. He is relentless at living out his belief that people are the most important part of any team and organization.

I believe that any of my success at building lasting relationships has been a result of the times I have been privileged to spend with Roger, observing and talking about what makes people, and teams, and organizations successful.

Cathi Shaw, Learning and Development Specialist, Worthington Industries, Inc.

Roger Campbell has leveraged in his book *It's About People* his vast experience, wisdom, and deep understanding of the value of people he gained from being a coach and athletic director at the collegiate level, and a 30-year illustrious career in leadership with Worthington Industries, Inc., as an Operations Manager, National Sales Manager, and the Director of Corporate Training and Development. Roger challenges those who read this book to more wisely invest in people. He makes the case that marketplace success is determined by how well an organization invests in their people. His easy-to-understand and practical methods in developing effective management skills to more effectively engage people to perform to their potential should better prepare the reader to make a wiser investment in the people who look to them for leadership. It is noteworthy in building his case that while your competitors may replicate processes, methods, technological equipment and facilities, etc., competitive advantage is gained when great managers know how to effectively connect their people to the business strategy.

Make an investment in yourself, read this book, and get ready to grow yourself and the people who depend on you for leadership!

Fred Crum, President, Personnel Profiles, Inc., Columbus

Roger Campbell has taken 53 years of content and put it into a practical and effective tool with *It's About People*. With so much focus being placed on the rapid changes in technology, this book is a great tool for young managers and a reminder (for executives) that without good people our organizations would not exist. The exercises with each chapter give us a chance to "look in the mirror" and test ourselves on our values, principles, and beliefs.

Jim Tyznik, Corporate Director of Human Resources, MPW Industrial Services

Roger's book reminded me of the countless hours I spent being coached and mentored by him. Every large corporation has a training department that offers training ... people are reluctant to participate. The time spent with Roger was different as he made it fun, enjoyable, and offered real-life experience.

I want to thank him for helping me transition from an hourly laborer to upper management with a 38-year international career.

Andy Bostik, Owner and President, Boz-Stix

Introduction

Ever since 1965 I have enjoyed working with people. I have always believed that people are the heart and soul of this country. Guess I learned that from my parents as a kid growing up. My mother and dad believed that people—all people—contributed to our society. I was fortunate in the fact that all my friends and their families felt the same. I was raised in this culture. I wanted to help people be the best so they could be good contributors. Over the years I have learned that all of us—you and me included—cannot be anything we want to be. However, we all can maximize the talents given us and be the best of whatever our role might be. This is an important point and I want to emphasize it now at the beginning: all job roles are important, and every job plays a part in the completion and success of company endeavors. Unfortunately, some managers don't understand the value of people and they choose to treat people like machines. Another discovery was that some people are satisfied with who they are and what they are and are not willing to change much to better themselves. My experience, though, has been that most people who get up and go to work each day really do want to do a good job, have fun doing it, and then return safely home to be with their loved ones. They want to work at a good company.

This book covers some of my thoughts about leadership, management, engagement, safety, enjoying people, and profitable growth.

I have been fortunate to have 53 years of experience (mostly great experiences), and I want to draw from these and pass on ideas to those in the early stages of their leadership journey. It is important for leaders to be able to really make a connection with their people to their organization's business strategy. I have always been an advocate of continual learning, and I want to make this book available to and for all those who want to learn. One of the best ways to learn is by experience, either by having it happen to us (reactionary) or by having some advanced knowledge of what is going to potentially happen and having ideas about how to manage the situation (proactive). Being prepared can lessen and perhaps help avoid unfortunate things from happening and will make the journey a lot more enjoyable for you and the people around you. This book is to be a proactive resource for the reader. All the topics and experiences mentioned in these chapters are actual happenings that I think may help others be successful.

There is a story I heard one time that goes like this: "Golf—it is a simple game. You have some clubs, you have a ball, and there is a 4-inch-deep hole. All a golfer must do is swing the club, hit the ball, and put the ball in the hole." Sounds simple, doesn't it? However, it is not always easy. There are sand traps, trees, and water, wind, hills/valleys, and players' attitudes. This list is what makes a simple game not so easy.

Management is also simple. You have a job, you have people, and there is a job goal or expectation. However, along the way you have workplace culture, people's behaviors, unclear expectations, safety/health issues, hiring/retention issues, suppliers and customers, waste and accidents. All of a sudden it is not simple. It becomes difficult. Every day and every week is like a white-water rafting trip. Calm, smooth, then boiling white water, rocks and narrow, dangerous passages, lots of water in the face, a pumping heart, calm again, smooth again—then catch your breath. Your attitude and preparation for each of those experiences determines how you react and respond, and the same is true of all the experiences you will have working with and leading people.

My hope is that you will find ideas within this book that will help you prepare for your "white-water rafting trip called leadership."

> *"I believe that people (the right people) are the one and only sustainable asset that any organization has. It is about hiring the right person, developing that individual, and then using great management methods to engage employees and profitably grow the business."*

— *Roger Campbell*

Acknowledgments

Many thanks to the following for their help and guidance along my life journey:

Mother and Dad: They taught me to respect and value others and the extreme importance of time, organization, and planning.

Sharon, my wife, who showed me that helping others is a fantastic calling, and it is enjoyable watching others accomplish their dreams.

Our Children, who were my motivation to be a positive role model.

Dr. Harold Kaser, my father-in-law: He mentored me in Compassion and caring of others.

Mr. Ed Sherman, Dr. Harold Bury, and Dr. Joe Fusco (Hall of Fame coaches and educators): They impressed upon me the fact that details and small things matter, expectations and consequences are necessary for growth, and hard work is a necessity for success.

Mr. John H. McConnell (Founder of Worthington Industries): Always emphasized that no matter where you are in life, you have only scratched the surface. Tomorrow lies ahead—make something of it. The Golden Rule is a great way to run an organization and one's life.

Thank you for the opportunities you provided.

All of the assistant coaches, players, employees, supervisors, managers, fellow trainers, friends, and customers that have taught me the importance of people in all of life's endeavor. (Unfortunately there are way too many to mention for fear of leaving someone off the list.) Your kindness and respect have made work not work, but a real enjoyment. I am so proud to have been included as your friend.

Thanks to you all! I have had a great life because of you and people like you who truly believe in the importance of People.

How to Use This Book

Just reading these chapters is only part of learning and improving. Experience has taught me that to really learn and grow I had to do something—not just think and talk about things, but actually do something. This book is all about basics. There is nothing in these pages that is earthshaking or totally new information. However, I can promise you that if you do something with these lessons, you will be well on your way to success as a leader. Included with each chapter is an exercise sheet to be used to stimulate questions, ideas, and challenges to help the reader actually **Go and Do something** with the knowledge and ideas. Share the exercise sheets with others, try ideas, and formulate strategies to help you and all those around you. I challenge the reader to just follow through and take action.

People

Every business that I'm aware of requires people to get things accomplished. It does not matter if it is a small company, mid-sized, or large, they all require someone to open up, to start equipment, answer the phone or check e-mails, to order or stock supplies, make or do, ship or send, shut down—you see what I mean. Not much gets accomplished unless there is someone to do it. All business has or needs money, people, time, technology/equipment, space, and a product or service. Depending on the kind of product or service and size of business, these 6 items play an important role in the success and long-term sustainability of the endeavor.

It is all about people. People are all different, and one of your most important roles as a business leader will be to attract and acquire the talented people needed in order to be successful and do the things necessary to keep them engaged and retained in your business. Good managers/leaders must be able to connect the value of their people to the business strategy of their organization. Over my years I have seen companies fail or be less than they should be because they do not pay close enough attention to the people side of their business. I believe Lee Iacocca (former chief of Chrysler) was right when he said, "Business is nothing more than a lot of human relationships." Many fail because they do not clearly define job roles, so consequentially they don't hire the right person for a job. They don't make it clear to the employee what their specific job requirements are, so employees get frustrated and the necessary things don't get done. They don't let the employee know how they are doing—good or bad—so improvement doesn't happen. They don't value the employee, so the employees just leave and go to another business where they are valued. Things don't just happen, but too many managers assume that when they hire someone, that person will somehow know what to do or will learn what has to be done.

The best managers I have worked for or with have been detail people. Nothing is left to chance. The good managers know why they hire someone and what they expect from them, and they communicate constantly so that nothing is forgotten or missed. The good managers make sure that every employee knows what is expected of them every day when they come to work and that all employees have the correct tools and supplies to do the job properly. After all of this is done, the good manager steps back and allows the employee to do their thing. If employees don't get this information it is difficult for them to be successful; they get frustrated, stressed out, and eventually if the situation is not corrected, will leave. This is a real losing situation. A loss for the organization because excessive turnover is a financial burden. A loss for customer confidence and retention. A loss for employees because of undue stress.

Many young managers are not prepared in how to work with people to get things accomplished. Many times managers fail because they believe their title somehow gives them the ability to pull power plays. The job title is something given to a person by the company to describe their role. A title, however, does not give that individual any power. The power for a manager comes from the people, and it is given to someone that the team sees as deserving. Someone who values people, someone who listens, someone who truly cares about people, someone who treats others with respect and dignity, and someone who can set a clear vision and can develop a positive culture.

So what is your view of people? How you see them and what you believe about them will be one of the factors that will determine your success or failure as a leader. Do you view employees as a necessary evil, or do you see them as one of the "Key" components to company success? Do you see them as the one "sustainable asset available to you that can continue to increase in value every day"? Many studies show that the leader and her/his opinions about employees is responsible for approximately 70–75% of employee productivity, engagement, and sustainable organizational growth. These factors also drive customer satisfaction, profitability, and how a company is viewed in the larger community. High-performing employees have 3 things in common: talent, engagement, and longevity with a company.

Your company is your people and your people are your company. Your task as the leader is to get them both aligned.

People Exercise Sheet

1. Identify several leaders I have known or worked for who I consider to be "top-notch."

   _____

   _____

2. What were their views about their employees and people in general? Why do these have meaning to me?

   _____

   _____

3. What from the above would I like to emulate in my career? Why?

   _____

   _____

4. How will I use this knowledge to connect the value of our people to the business strategy of the organization (my plan)?

   _____

   _____

Values and You

What do you stand for and why? This is a very important piece of the puzzle to your success as a manager/leader of people. If you are asking employees to give you their valuable time and effort (blood, sweat, and tears), your customers to give you their business (trust and money), you must as a person and a company have a set of values that show who you are and what you believe to be important. These values must be on display every day for all to see. I believe values are like magnets—they can attract employees and customers and will allow you to create a powerful community of energized and engaged people.

Values define for us what we stand for and what is important. Values are nonnegotiable. They are not to be used just when we want to, or when we think they can help. Values define you and your company. They are an outward example of who you really are as a person or company. They are obvious to others because they are out there for all to see. Values will be the foundational building blocks of your culture and are powerful forces that will guide you and your company. They act as boundaries within which you and the company will operate in pursuit of your vision. Some people I have worked with over the years have even called values their code of conduct. Jon M. Huntsman in his book *Winners Never Cheat* says this about values: "Values provide us with ethical water wings whose deployment is as critical in today's wave tossed corporate boardrooms as they were in yesterday's classrooms."

There is a simple exercise I love to play with new managers/leaders to help them understand values. Not sure where we got this, but it works. Begin by giving each person 5 sticky notes. Ask them to write an important personal value on each note that is really important to them, such as personal health, financial security, family togetherness, continual learning, community service, etc. They place the sticky notes in front of them and then through a series of questions you ask, they will arrive at their number 1 value. As a young leader it is important to know what your values are and why they are important to you. These will be your guide posts or curbs in life. This exercise will take a lot of self-reflection. Take it seriously—remember these are your building blocks. The world will see them and know what they are, because these values will help you make all the important decisions in your life.

You should do a similar exercise with your senior leadership team. You must decide what are going to be the values that your company will hold to be of utmost importance. These values will tell all who you are and what you believe about people, customers, work, and community. The company values are the building blocks of the company culture. These values should be talked about every day with everyone you come in contact with. They will become the guides that all employees use to make company decisions. The culture you develop and promote will tell everyone what you believe about employees, what you think about the importance of customers, what are your views about your supply chain partners, what you think about the company and its involvement in the community. Your personal values and your company values which determine your culture are vital to the long-term success of you and the company. Don't pick values because they sound good—pick them because you and the company sincerely believe they are real values that you can and will support every day.

There should never be a day you as a leader don't think about or act on the company culture. Every day you must work for alignment in the organization on the culture. Break down the company silos and work to have all within the company make decisions based on the values and culture of the company, not for the good of a few individuals or one department. If you are successful you will help produce sustainability for the organization. When hiring people for your company, it is important that they believe in the company values. If not it will be difficult to reach alignment.

Values Exercise Sheet

1. Take time and reflect on what are the top 5 values in my life and why they are important.

    _____

    _____

2. How do others know these values are important to me?

    _____

    _____

3. Do I really know who I am?

    _____

    _____

Values in Action

Several years before "employee engagement" became a talking point in boardrooms everywhere, an associate and I had the opportunity to work with a group of young managers whose fresh ideas on workplace culture still resonate today. These six managers, who were developing and building a new manufacturing company, were convinced that if they had the "right culture" they not only could build a great organization, but also one that could be sustained for many years.

In addition to making a great product, they also knew that if they were to be successful, they needed all employees to believe in and see this new company as *theirs*. They wanted all employees to behave and act as entrepreneurs. They wanted the employees to worry about the quality of the final product, to have "direct line of sight with the customer," and to be concerned about each other's safety. They truly wanted the company to be like a family.

They were convinced that if the company was to be successful, they would need a philosophy of management allowing every employee to be deeply involved in the company. They coined the phrase "Hire for values and train for skills" and were able to expound upon their management values by developing the simple acronym **C.H.A.T.**

- C – Courage

- H – Honesty

- A – Attitude

- T – Trust

The new philosophy became laser focused and was present every-where, from banners to pre-shift meetings under the encouraging slo-gan *"Let's Have a C.H.A.T."*

COURAGE

They wanted everyone to understand that they, as managers, were going to stand up for the company values, and expected others to do the same, even if it wasn't the popular choice. They emphasized that even though other competitors abide by the status quo, employees and managers were encouraged to take risks, because without risks there would be no progress.

Courage was also found by looking out for each other. They believed it was easy to stay silent and allow standards to slip, but it took cour-age to make sure everyone wore safety glasses and wore the proper PPE.

As managers, they displayed courage by allowing themselves to be vulnerable. They clearly understood that they had the authority of the company, but they also wanted the power of the people. The manag-ers did not have to make all the decisions, nor did they have to okay every purchase. They allowed the people to think and act as owners.

HONESTY

They also believed in the value of honesty, and they wanted to hire people who lived by that same value. Honesty is a simple concept, but one that affects every facet of your organization. They simply guided their employees to remember that there are no secrets; you should share your information with others so that everyone can make the right decisions. Avoid being misleading or deceptive, and always do what you say you are going to do.

Simply put, "just tell the truth."

ATTITUDE

Each one of these managers used the term "look in the mirror," meaning that the team's attitude is the reflection of the manager's.

If you want others to be positive, then you must be positive. If you want people to care about others, then you as managers need to care about others. If you want employees to be concerned about quality and customer service, then they as managers had to demonstrate the same concerns.

They knew that an environment of positive people is necessary to be successful. The management team realized that one's attitude may be the only thing in life under their control, but that their attitudes can greatly affect the emotions, behaviors, and responses of everyone they come into contact with. Their family, their fellow employees, the customers and the community.

Knowing this, they fully encouraged employees to interact with customers and external vendors. Not only did this encourage more positive attitudes, but it spread the word to current and future customers: "**This is a great company**." Employees felt they could make a positive difference, and so they did. Everyone was engaged.

TRUST

After a strong focus on courage, honesty, and attitude, the management team knew that something else was needed to hold their organization together—they decided on trust. Trust was the glue that holds all relationships together, and it would be the glue that would hold their new organization, and their "family," together.

As a group they determined what trust would look like in the real day-to-day life of the company, in both the form of a noun and a verb.

Trust as a noun was a responsibility placed on everyone—management and team. They knew they had to be trustworthy in every aspect of their business if they expected the others to trust them and ultimately reflect their values.

And *trust* as a verb was an outward example, obvious to everyone, of how they thought about the team. They trusted team members to do the right things, they trusted everyone to not just pass the buck, and they showed trust by sharing financial numbers with the team and trusted in their ideas by asking them to come up with ways to improve quality, production, and reduce unnecessary cost.

The new young managers were convinced that if the company cared about the success of their employees, and the employees cared about the success of the company, they would have a winner. They wanted a symbiotic or mutually beneficial relationship. And they and their company culture are still thriving under these simple yet focused values today.

"The behavior that best creates credibility and inspires trust is acting in the best interest of others." — Steven M. R. Covey

Values in Action Exercise Sheet

1. What are 3 lessons learned from this story?

    ▪

    ▪

    ▪

2. How will I be able to use each one to build a better culture for my work team or company?

    _____

    _____

3. Who else on the Team should read this story?

    _____

    _____

4. Can I prepare a brief 2-minute presentation on my values?

    _____

    _____

Lessons Learned

Sometimes our lessons come from places or people we least expect to be coaching us. I want to share with you one such example. I learned a lot from being with my grandparents. The following 4 Leadership Principles I learned from my grandmother have played a role in who I am. These lessons still have meaning in 2018.

Having grown up in the mid- to late '40s, I was fortunate to have a close relationship with my maternal grandparents. Back in those days it was much different than today and the relationship I had with my grandparents was a thing of joy. We lived in different communities, there were no cell phones or Internet, and travel was somewhat restricted. My grandparents were farmers and Wildcat oil-well drillers. They worked extremely hard for what they had, but never once did I hear them complain about anything. Every summer from the age of 8, I would visit the farm for 3 weeks, and it was the most enjoyable time of the summer. During those visits I helped my grandparents do the chores, and I was able to observe how they did things and what they said. At the time I did not realize that I was being coached by them. They did not sit me down and drill me, or make me take notes. They just allowed me to observe them, their behaviors and attitudes. This helped develop my values.

Grandma would always tell me, "**Don't put off the weeding of the garden till tomorrow. It might rain tomorrow and we will not be able**

to get our work done." What a lesson. How many times do we put off till tomorrow that important sales call, or the necessary discussion with an employee about safety or quality? Many times when we put things off till tomorrow, the sale is lost to a competitor or an injury occurs because of a careless act. It is very important for employees to have a sense of urgency. Tomorrow will always come and it will be filled with lots of challenges—take care of today. As the leader you must demonstrate a sense of urgency. Your employees will see this and know it is important. Always talk about the importance of taking care of today. If supervisors see an employee not wearing safety glasses on the plant floor, they must approach the employee in a helpful manner and explain the safety reasons for wearing the glasses. If this opportunity is missed there is potential for loss of eyesight.

Talk with the rural route mailman every day: My grandmother would always wait for the mailman to stop at the mailbox. It happened every day at 12:30 pm. It was the time Grandmother would be able to catch up on all the news from the area. The mailman talked to all the people on his route. He knew who was under the weather, who was going to get married, or who had a son that was going to ship out to Germany. If someone down the road needed something, my grandparents could take a pie or lend a hand. Communication with others was their lifeblood. It was instant news—or at least within several hours. That brief 2- to 3-minute discussion helped my grandparents feel connected to the others in the community. One of the important keys of getting employees engaged is to help them feel like they are in the know. Let employees know about the new customer coming on board, or the new technology that is being considered, or new equipment that is being purchased. The more information that people have, the better decisions they can make. Good communication is a tool for learning and connecting. Good leaders must be good communicators. McKinsey Global states that "productivity improves 20–25% in organizations with connected employees."

Tell Mr. Martin that you only want 5 chunks of cheese: Mr. Martin was the owner of a small grocery store in the community. He was also a farmer, so the store was only open at certain times of the day, or if you knocked on his door for emergency needs. My grandparents never needed to buy much because they provided most of their needs from their own efforts. However, when they did need something my grandmother would send me to the store (about ½ mile away) with very specific instructions on how many slices, chunks, or scoops of goods to buy. Grandmother used to say "waste not, want not." They did not have any of our modern conveniences, so there was no excessive up-front buying. She called it being thrifty, but in reality they were practicing the concept of Lean Thinking long before it became the norm. They only bought exactly what they needed. There was no waste. They had no massive inventory of goods. Everything on their farm had a place, and that is exactly where you would find it if needed. As a leader you must be teaching your team about being lean. Share with others the cost of wasted inventory, wasted movement, or damaged material that is being stored. Everyone must understand that these costs can't be passed off to the customer. Congratulate groups that practice lean processes and share the success stories with the rest of the organization. Introduce the 6-S process in the office and on the plant floor (Sort/Set in order/Shine/Standardize/Sustain/Safety). Require a planning and a debriefing process. Discuss with the team the concept of value-added activity. If you do, everyone will get better. It is your job as a leader to do this. Everyone in the organization has a fiduciary responsibility to the company—everyone.

It's Time for a picnic: On the last Saturday evening before I would go home, there would always be a family picnic. It was a big celebration for me, my family, my relatives, and the local neighbors. As I think back on it food was always a big part of life on the farm. The celebrations were always special—lots of stories, good jokes, games, and just good fun. My grandparents knew the value of celebrations and the comradery that happened each time they built a bonfire. They did not call it "team building." It was just a picnic or a wiener roast, but they were developing a sense of belonging in the family and the community. Abraham Maslow identified the sense of belonging to be one of the 5 levels of motivation that he stressed as being important in the hierarchy of motivation. If employees feel like they belong, they will have a tendency to be much more engaged. Work to create a sense of workplace family. It will help create a caring, cooperating teamwork culture. At every picnic as the fire died down and every-one was gathered around (young and old), there was always a history story about the community or some family member that had done something special. It was one of the ways that family and community values were passed down from one generation to another. As a lead-er you can and must share important stories about company heroes and those that have made it possible for everyone to have a job. Ask others to share their stories about the company and its heroes and heroines. Your company values are important pieces of the company culture. You can call them "philosophy stories" or "cultural stories"— whatever you call them, know their value to the development and engagement of your team. These are the perfect way to let everyone know your values and your expectations, and it gives all a chance to feel like they belong.

As many authors have stated, leadership is an art and not a science. Create your own art by taking important pieces of people's lives and using them to build a place where people want to work. Leadership is not easy, but it can be one of the most rewarding accomplishments in your life. I hope these lessons learned from my grandparents will help you be successful.

There is a picture hanging in my office of a pack of running horses that has the caption: "**The speed of the leader determines the rate of the pack**." I truly believe that the leader can do this. It can't be phony or false excitement. It has to be a belief that comes from the gut and heart if it is to really help effectively lead others.

Lessons Learned Exercise Sheet

1. Who are some individuals I have learned from over the years?

    ▪

    ▪

    ▪

2. What leadership lessons do I remember from their mentoring?

    ▪

    ▪

    ▪

3. Am I a continual learner? If not, why?

    _____

    _____

4. What was the last business book I read, or when was the last seminar or class I attended?

    ▪   Book:

    ▪   Seminar or class:

5. Am I mentoring others? What is good about mentoring?

_____

_____

6. Do I encourage others to be continual learners?

_____

_____

You Are the Coach

Recently I had an enlightening lunch with a friend from college. We had both participated in sports, played on the same football team, and learned from a National Collegiate Football Hall of Fame coach. Coincidentally, we're both active in the profession of business consulting and mentoring of management team members.

While we were discussing the different issues business leaders deal with and are asking for, we suddenly stopped, looked at each other, and said, "Hey, this is basic football!"

We realized that the actions needed to create corporate success are the same basic tactics we saw used to make us successful as college athletes. Which got me thinking: how many principles that make football players and coaches great can also be applied to being great in business?

ATTITUDE IS EVERYTHING

Successful individuals, whether they're coaches or business leaders, quite often have much in common. They possess enthusiasm, have meaningful relationships with many around them, they're hard workers and they produce results. In short, they're winners.

They know the importance of personal image and good communication, and that planning and setting goals is also a must. They constantly evaluate everything, including themselves and their impact. They celebrate the now, but always plan for tomorrow. And they care like crazy for the team and give back to the community.

This is just a sliver of what can make a coach successful, but know that business requires the same. How do you stack up against this list? If your attitude isn't conveying these attributes, then you could be looking at a losing season in your business.

POWER OF THE PLAYERS

In college sports there is much-needed emphasis on recruiting the best players that fit your values and have the skills that are necessary to excel in your team's systems or schemes.

In college, the coaches do all of the recruiting, and they don't turn over this responsibility to others. And for an important reason—coaches want to get to really know the players and their family members. They use this time to focus beyond the player's stats and evaluate how the new player will fit with the team and how they will react to coaching and discipline. Good recruiting is vital to the success of the program.

In the business world, it is about finding employees who share your company values, fit into the culture, and possess an attitude which will allow them to be flexible and care about customers and the business. Just like a great coach is present to get firsthand insight into each potential player, managers and supervisors must insist on being part of the hiring process to bring in the best for the team.

Many successful companies will even expand on this practice and will involve hourly team members in the interviewing process to ensure that the new employee will properly "fit" with the current team.

I believe team makeup is one of the keys to success and is crucial in keeping things in sync. The philosophy of hiring for attitude and then training for skills is an excellent path to follow. Much like football, good recruiting of engaged employees is vital to the success of any business.

BE YOUR BRAND

Coaches and their staff have an offensive and defensive scheme or style of play. This is what they are known for; this is what they believe in. Their particular style is what attracts the kind of players they need to be successful—it's their brand.

Are they wide open, constantly attacking and challenging the defense, or are they controlled? Do they blitz a lot and constantly try to beat the opponent with "tricky" and multiple looks, or do they let the opponent know they are in for a real knock-down, drag-out fight? These distinctions in style will determine how the team is regarded by everyone from players to rivals to fans.

Like a style of play, businesses have a distinct brand and company culture. It's very important for the organization to let all employees, customers, and suppliers know what the organization stands for to be noticed, be competitive, and bring in the best. It is essential to concentrate on company culture: it communicates to the employee and customer their value and importance to the organization. If you don't have a brand, or you don't like your current brand, then it's never too late to rewrite your signature plays to make your company what you want it to be.

Coaches need to communicate with many different groups. From newspaper and TV reporters to other faculty members and alumni groups, and most of all, they need to communicate with their staff, team, trainers, and equipment personnel. For a business built on physicality, correctly communicating the right message to the right group is just as important as running plays.

Coaches believe it is important to get the message to everyone, but they also know that a significant part of communication is listening. The great coaches will keep their ears and minds open to the same people they communicate with regularly—always ready to embrace a better way of doing things.

In business, leaders also understand the importance of clear, thorough, and frequent communication. No matter whether you're a coach or a business leader, you must communicate from your heart and your gut; your sincerity will show through and you'll get results.

Start each day with a "team huddle" or pre-shift "soapbox" where you talk about the challenges of the day with the entire staff. Remind everyone that it is important to meet production needs, but it must be done in a safe manner. Discuss where the team stands on quality issues, and in general make sure that everyone is fit for duty.

In football each play starts with a huddle. Everyone knows the play, the formation, the snap count, and other important information prior to leaving the huddle. The QB makes sure everyone is on the same page. Shift leaders must do the same if they want every member to be on the same page about production, safety, quality, and behaviors. Communication, Communication, Communication.

EVALUATE EVERY ANGLE, BUT BE FLEXIBLE

Coaches are paranoid about evaluation. They evaluate everything from the kind of shoes worn, to the length of time to release a pass, to blocking performance. They film practice and games and spend hours evaluating down and distance tendencies, position or field tendencies, if the offensive guard took the correct first step, or the exact location of the ball in the carrier's hand prior to being tackled. To many these seem like small and inconsequential items. But it is these basics that win football games, and coaches know that the team that makes the fewest mistakes will win. They also know that they and the team must be flexible enough to make changes on the fly.

If something is not working, then you just can't keep doing the same thing and expect that sometime soon you will get lucky. Being flexible is the result of constant communication with the team about being flexible, and always being prepared with a backup play or scheme that everyone is familiar with. Coaches understand they are being evaluated not just every season, but also every week. So do you have an evaluation plan? Great leaders are always comparing what *should be happening* to what is *actually happening*. If those are always the same then that is fantastic, but if the two are going in a different direction then there is a gap in the goal.

You must immediately start the questioning process: **W**hat is happening? **W**here is it happening? **W**ho is it happening to? **W**hen is it happening? **W**hy is it happening? (5 Ws.) Many leaders use a simple SWOT analysis or a quarterly measurement report. Today's technology, if programmed correctly, should give the manager of today much information and data to review to begin the questioning process of managing the gap between what is expected and what is actually happening. Whatever you use, make sure you are honest with yourself and learn from the results. If you don't you are cheating everyone—the employees, the customers, the organization, and yourself.

You Be the Coach Exercise Sheet

1. If I were on the outside of the company looking in, what would I
    see? What would I identify as the "Brand"?

    _____

    _____

2. Am I and other managers and supervisors actively involved in the
    interviewing process?

    _____

    _____

3. Do I and others have a good understanding of the term "job fit"?

    _____

    _____

4. Have I ever tried any kind of pre-shift meetings?

    _____

    _____

5. What are the advantages of a pre-shift session?

    _____

    _____

Don't Derail Your Career

Some leaders seem to always do or say things which cause others in the company to stand back, scratch their head, and say "what is that?" If the situations happen frequently enough or are disruptive to the rest of the team, the offending person will suffer and their career will be derailed. If the situations are not corrected, the offending person may not be around. Let's take a brief look at some of the issues I have seen derail a person's career.

Lack of self-awareness: Not knowing or understanding how you are perceived by others or how your behaviors and actions affect others. One group of managers I worked with described it as looking in the mirror every day. Are you seen as being sincere, and a straight shooter? Phony people are easily recognized and are avoided like the plague. Knowing who you are, how others see you, and how your behaviors affect others is a key competence for leaders.

Not willing to ask for help or coaching: Most people understand the importance of asking others for help. Maybe it is as simple as getting different ideas or a different way of approaching difficult situations; it is always good to ask others' opinions. The managers that get in trouble seem to be the ones that always want to go it alone. Don't be afraid to ask for help—it does not mean you are a poor leader.

Body Hygiene and Dress: It is important to keep clean and neat and the manager must set the standard. Dress must always match the work environment and company standard. When dealing with customers, it is important to remember how they perceive you and what their expectations are. People that work in close proximity with others or have contact with customers must always take into consideration the effect of their hygiene on others. This is part of self-awareness. Enough said.

Always late for meetings/or not ending on time: This gives the impression you don't care about others or their time requirements. Everyone is busy and wants to be respected. By starting and ending on time, you not only show you are organized but that you respect others.

Always on your phone/buried in your laptop: These behaviors actually become barriers between you and others. It makes you unapproachable, and if you seem unapproachable what value do you bring?

Cursing/using bad language: This behavior is offensive to employees and many times they think the cursing is directed at them. This behavior is one that causes employees to disrespect their manager.

Wearing inappropriate clothing: It is important to understand the culture where you work. Dress should be geared to what is the acceptable standard according to the culture. As a manager/leader you should always set the standard that you want from everyone.

Unethical or dishonest behavior: This is seen as being disrespectable and that you as a leader cannot be trusted. Not only will this cause you to lose the respect of the team, but it will probably cost you your career. Of course lying and stealing are two of the biggest sins one can commit. Above all you must be ethical or you will have no credibility.

Not following up in a timely manner: This is a sign of disrespect, lack of organization, and is perceived as you really don't care. Employees just want an answer to their questions, and you as the manager owe it to them. Make sure to take time to clearly explain the reasons for the decision. It may not be the answer they want, but it shows that you respect them enough to consider the question and give them an honest answer. Use whatever works for you to record questions asked by your team so as not to forget. At the end of each day, check this list to remind you of what still needs follow-up responses. For years I have carried a small 3x5 spiral notepad. It was easy to carry in a jacket or pant pocket, and was easily accessible to pull out and write down the question in front of the person asking. When they saw me write it down, they knew I was going to follow up and I respected their questions and opinions.

Not willing to help others, Not a team player: A primary competency for all leaders is to make sure you remove the barriers that make it difficult for others to do their jobs. One of the most frustrating issues to employees is not having the proper tools, equipment, or supplies to do the job safely, quickly, and with quality. Make sure that as a leader you spend time with the team to make sure they have what they need. If you do, you not only gain their respect, but the customer will also see it in the end-product quality. It is as simple as asking, "Do you have the tools necessary to do your job?" Some young managers are willing to throw team members "under the bus" just to protect their own position because they have not taken the necessary steps to remove as many barriers as possible.

Not a continual learner: If you are not staying current with new technology or business processes, you will fall behind and eventually become a dinosaur. Business trends, technology, customer ideas are ever changing, and if you as the leader are not staying ahead or current with these, you and your organization will suffer. Do you know as much about your customer's customer as possible? A phrase that I agree with is "Leaders are readers," and I have always tried to read an article or do some kind of daily learning. Jamie Dimon, CEO of J.P. Morgan Chase, says that he begins every day by reading 4–5 newspapers. He is also a fan of asking questions of other businesspeople and then really listening to what they say. This is how he tries to continually improve and grow his organization. It may be as simple as talking to a store clerk about technology in the store and how it helps make things quicker or easier for customers. It is a great way to learn how people think and understand what is important to them.

It is more than just reading. Get out and take a class or seminar, get involved in local groups that will challenge you, network and communicate with many different people. Jim Rohm, the author and motivational speaker, says, "searching and learning is where the miracle process begins." It could also be said: if you aren't learning you are dying.

"I am the boss" attitude: This derailer is the one that gets a lot of new managers. Don't let your position go to your head. Don't get caught in the trap that you are the only one that knows what to do, and don't act as if you have everyone under your thumb. The team will see you as arrogant and will be waiting for you to make a mistake. You will not be seen as the leader, but as an intimidator. This type of behavior will make it very difficult to build lasting and meaningful relationships.

Not able to admit mistakes: Good leaders must be able to admit that they made a mistake. This is one of the things that will help create trust in your team. Some leaders think it makes them look weak if they admit a mistake. Actually it is just the opposite: the team will have a much greater respect for the leader and trust will flourish. To put it another way, the leader must be transparent.

Not willing to give time to others: This comes across to the team as "you don't really care about us." One mistake that people make is to ask someone, "How are you?" Then they don't stop and take the time to listen. When that happens, it comes across as just playing the role or a lack of real sincerity.

Lack of Consistency: Managers get derailed because they are not consistent. Many times their words do not match their actions. This causes a lack of trust. Often they are hot one day and cold the next. This causes employees to wonder: which boss will show up today? Both of these examples lead to lack of trust. Without trust you have nothing.

Derailing can happen to all of us if we are not vigilant. Stay aware and stay connected. Many times derailments happen when leaders put themselves on an island. Make it a point to "look in the mirror" on a regular basis and be honest with what you are seeing and hearing.

Don't Derail Your Career Exercise Sheet

1. Do I have the courage to stand in front of my team and admit a mistake?

    _____

    _____

2. Can I take constructive coaching from others if they think I am doing something that could derail my career?

    _____

    _____

3. Who do I turn to for honest feedback?

    _____

    _____

4. Has anyone ever told me I need to make changes in any of the areas mentioned in this chapter? If so, what did I do?

    _____

    _____

Setting the Expectations for Success – Parking Lots with Lines

A company that I was consulting with had a parking lot without marked spaces. Over the years the lines had become faded and in many instances they were totally missing. When the employees arrived at work, they would park in whichever manner seemed best to them and however they could squeeze their car into a spot. This was complicated by the fact of second shift trying to find parking before first shift had vacated the lot. As you can imagine, it was a mess. The employees were unhappy and the managers complained about how dumb the employees were acting.

As I began to work with the management, I tried to help them understand that the employees were not dumb, but merely needed lines to show them where to park. It did not take long and soon parking lines were painted on the blacktop, and instantly every employee parked in the correct direction and there were even spaces for visitors and vendors to park. The lot was laid out so there were fifteen extra spots, which allowed spaces for early arriving second-shift employees. It did not take long till everyone was pleased about the parking accommodations and a minor aggravation was eliminated.

Parking lines are valuable because they give us boundaries to make the job of parking easier. They serve to give order and eliminate chaos.

The same is true when employees have a clear understanding of their job. The Gallup survey, in measuring strong workplaces, identified as the number-one link to employee engagement, company profitability, employee retention, and productivity as "Do I know what is expected of me at work?" Employees that know what is expected of them at work don't work in a vacuum. Employees that know what is expected of them at work are more willing to accept responsibility for the quality and quantity of their work. When employees have a sense of direction and understand their role in the organization, they are better able to perform as a valuable asset. Listed below are a few things to keep in mind when thinking about employees and "knowing what is expected of them at work."

- **This begins early** – Job postings and interviewing must be very clear on what the job/jobs entail. What are the expectations and why does the position exist?

- **After the Hire** – It is important that the new employee, at any level of the organization, understands their role and what outcomes are expected. Again, make sure they know why the position exists. In other words, "Why do they get paid?" This really is the same as putting down lines in the parking lot.

- **Continuously** – Great managers are constantly involved with their reports. It is important to focus on removing roadblocks and barriers to help make the employee's job more doable. Give continuous feedback and provide support without removing responsibility. These feedback sessions help keep employees in the lines.

- **Train** – Training is not for fixing. Send talented employees to training to learn new skills and gain deeper insight and knowledge. With employees that do need to "be fixed," create a plan that focuses on the improvement needed and set

responsible time lines. Set expectations and explain consequences for not meeting expectations. Remember this does
not have to be confrontational, just clear and assertive.

- **The Manager** – Never lose your focus. Always, in every con-
versation and interaction, discuss the need for excellence and
foster an environment that encourages employee discretion-
ary effort. You and the company paint the lines, and the employee will park without a traffic cop being there to make
them do it.

- **Review** – Sometimes the lines in a parking lot need to be
moved or repainted. The same is true with job responsibilities. Customers may change, technologies and materials may
change, so it is necessary for the employee and the manager
to have good, open communication about the role of the job.
Change the role if it is required, but make sure your employee
has a clear understanding about the new role and explain the
why.

- **Celebrate** – It is important to thank team members for their accomplishments. Words like "thank you," "I appreciate that,"
"you really did a great job" are very meaningful and help you
show your appreciation for the work done. Remember that
you must be sincere. "Don't blow smoke up their shorts" is
a phrase to remember. People know when you are being sincere or if you are just pandering. Celebration also can be accomplished by giving the employee a new challenge or even
a promotion.

Great employees will perform well if they know what is expected
of them. To be a great manager, make sure every employee knows
exactly why they have a position and what they must do to be successful. These are the parking lines of the workplace. Make sure they

are there, make sure they are clear, and make sure they are changed if the business changes.

Great managers and great leaders know that one of their important jobs is to help paint the lines for employees. Everyone, in my opinion, needs boundaries or lines so they can function to their maximum.

Setting Expectations Exercise Sheet

1. Does everyone in my company understand their job role and its importance? Why do they get paid?

    _____

    _____

    How do I know?

    _____

    _____

2. In all of my conversations, do I stress the need for excellence?

    _____

    _____

3. Do I always thank my team for their hard work and accomplishments?

    _____

    _____

4. Do I always encourage everyone to review job expectations and make changes as required by customer needs?

    _____

    _____

Set Expectations
and Manage the Gap

One of the best leadership lessons I ever learned was to set expectations for the group. When I would set expectations it let everyone know what was important, what and how much had to be accomplished, and when it needed to be completed. All employees, from the newest person hired to the most senior executive, want to know what needs to be done to be successful. The Gallup Organization identified **not knowing what is expected of me at work** to be one of the issues that frustrate and keep employees from doing their best at work. Many times we make the mistake of thinking that once a person has a job they should know what to do, and when to do it. Actually the reverse is true. Many times we just let employees drift and try to figure out what must be done. We do this at the expense of time, quality, customer service, and employee engagement. Often if the employee does not get the information they get frustrated, angry, discouraged, and leave the company. When we have conducted exit interviews within some organizations with high turnover, we have found "lack of clear work expectations" is one of the top 3 reasons for leaving a company. Ninety-day performance evaluations are often given, and employees are rated on doing a job without ever really being given expectations about the job or any specific training. I believe expectations and goal setting are different. Expectations are what you as a manager think should happen. Goals are the plans of others to help make the expectations happen. Expectations are positive, specific, and precise times, quality, numbers, behaviors that express a desired finish. Setting these kinds of clear expectations is like looking at the picture on the front of a puzzle box. The picture is there to show what the end result will look like. Can you imagine putting together a 750-piece puzzle without this kind of help? That is exactly what employees feel when they try to do a job without training or clear expectations on numbers, quality, or other things.

WHY SET EXPECTATIONS?

As a leader/manager you must set clear expectations. Review the company values as a guide when you set these expectations. Expectations help to hold people accountable for their behaviors. The company values will help you establish the expectations for the company culture. How will we treat each other, what are the beliefs about customers/suppliers, why is this company important, and how should employees and company be involved in the community. You as the leader must paint the picture so others know what the end result will look like. In order to set clear expectations, you as the leader must have constant contact with customers, employees, community leaders, and your board of advisors. You will find it easier to set expectations after discussing with and listening to the above groups. Customers will tell you what they need as for the products/services your company provides. They will tell you about quality and service issues—good and bad. Customers will tell you what they think about you and your company. You must stay in constant contact with your employees. They are the heartbeat of the organization. If you have worked to establish good open communications with them, they will give you much of the information you need to set expectations for the company. They will give insights into good/bad frontline managers, they will tell you how to eliminate non-value-added activities, they will tell you what tools and equipment is needed, they will give you ways to make things safer. Just listen. After discussions with customers and employees, it is always helpful to do a strengths/weaknesses/opportunities/threats analysis (SWOT). Take time to digest the information and have follow-up discussions with all the groups or specific individuals. If you do the above, you will be doing one of the key responsibilities of a leader, which is *planning*: where do you want the company or unit to go, and how are they going to get there? You must also spend time with community leaders and find ways that you, your employees, and your company can be good citizens. Remember that you and your business are members of the larger community. How are you perceived? If you are not perceived as helping the community and its citizens, how can you expect the community to support you? Employees want to work for a company they can be proud of, so one thing you can do to attract good employees is to show them you are engaged in the community and you want employees to be engaged as well. There are many ways to be involved in the community—it just depends on you and your employees. Ask, ask, ask and listen, listen, listen. Maybe it is delivering meals on wheels, working at food pantries, sponsoring a food drive, helping mentor or teach others how to read or set budgets. I was fortunate to have been with Worthington Industries—a steel company—and we were able to do all of these things at many different locations around the U.S. . . . At the same time we were able to deliver on service and quality and were an extremely profitable company. It was because of the company leadership that set positive examples for all of us and encouraged all to be good citizens.

If you have a board or an advisory group you must spend time with them, encourage them to get to know your employees and to gain understanding about your customer base. Ask them strategic questions and encourage them to ask you the tough questions. They should want to know if everyone on the team has a clear understanding of what are the core competencies of the company. They should find out what your customers want and need. Keep the advisors engaged in your business if you want to get as much as you can from the relationship.

After expectations are communicated, the employees and other managers can then establish goals as to how they can accomplish the desired expectations. Expectations are set from above and goals are developed lower in the organization to help meet the company or unit expectations.

Manage the Gap Exercise Sheet

1. How can I help my team have direct line of sight with our customers and the community?

_____

_____

2. Do I and the other managers spend appropriate time with the employees, customers, community leaders, and advisors?

_____

_____

3. Can I and other managers lead an effective "SWOT" analysis?

_____

_____

4. Is our management team approachable?

_____

_____

Don't Wait Till Things Get Out of Control

A mistake made by some leaders is not addressing issues immediately. Many times they believe that issues will take care of themselves and no management actions are required. This might be true in some instances, but the majority of time effective leaders make decisions to "handle" the situations before they spiral out of control. Many people say, "Don't make a mountain out of a mole hill." Experience has shown the opposite is true: don't let a mole hill become a mountain. Effective leaders and managers are always "taking the temperature" of the organization. Effective leaders understand that "taking the temperature" means always communicating and listening to all internal and external issues in the organization. If a leader begins to hear about an issue that may have an effect on the company at any level, they have a responsibility to look into the situation themselves or request another with greater knowledge to look into the situation. This does not mean the leader will have to make changes or correct every situation, but it does mean they are responsible for the smooth, safe, and profitable operation of the organization.

A former mentor once told a group of us that issues—good and bad— are like seeds in the ground. As they grow through the surface of the ground they show as a sprout, if left to grow they become a stalk, and if left to grow even more they become a tree. The analogy is that as soon as something appears, the leader must evaluate: is it going to be good for the organization, or will it be bad for the organization? If good, it needs to be nurtured and cared for, so it will grow and become a positive influence. If it seems to be a bad thing, it needs to be handled quickly before it becomes a sprout, a stalk, or a tree. Leaders need to be constantly taking the temperature of the operation. Is there someone in the group that is doing something unsafe? Then the leader must step in and stop the behavior so the individual or others will not be harmed. Is there a quality or production issue that is going to negatively affect product or service to the end user? If so, the leader must step in and find out the reasons and help the team work for a positive correction. Is there someone in the office or the plant floor abusing or harassing others? If so, the leader must step in and find out what is going on. Speak with all parties involved and work with them to make the necessary changes to correct the situation. As a leader you just can't wave your hand and assume change will happen. Change, if possible, must come from the people involved. A good process I once learned is: **1.** Sit down with the individual/s and describe the situation you are seeing. This is important to have a clear and accurate place from where to begin the process. Make sure that the discussion is focused on the behavior/s that are having a negative effect and do not attack the individual. **2.** Ask the individual why this is happening. Listen, Listen. **3.** Ask the individual if they have a plan that could fix the situation. Listen to their plan without interjecting your thoughts and give them time to lay it out. Ask questions to help clarify their plan, and then make any suggestions that may help them be successful. Remember, the important thing here is it is their plan, and the majority of people will work harder to support their own plan than they will to support another's plan. **4.** Set a specific date, location, and time for a follow-up to see how their plan is working. The length of time till the follow-up will depend upon the seriousness of the issue and the complexity of the plan. However, don't wait too long to follow up. You must stay actively involved to show the employee that you really do care about the issue and its effect on the group or organization. If the plan does not seem to be working, then is the time when you as the leader must step in and make suggestions on what should be done (expectations) and set consequences—positive for improvement or negative if improvement does not take place. According to Dr. Morris Massey, "without consequences there will be no behavioral modification." Once you have established expectations and consequences, it is then in the hands of the individual/s that must make the behavioral change. The follow-up meetings are key to the success of bringing about any behavioral change, and as Gordon Jackson, author of *Coaches Encourage and Bosses Punish*, says, "it is a universally recognized truth that few modify their behaviors unless consequences are attached." It should also be emphasized that situations must be handled in a timely fashion, and waiting can often make things worse.

Don't Wait Exercise Sheet

1. Do I feel comfortable having difficult discussions with others, or do I see them as potential conflicts?

   _____

   _____

2. Can I have difficult discussions without yelling and screaming?

   _____

   _____

3. Do I know all my fellow employees well enough that I feel comfortable discussing issues with them? If not, how can I correct this situation?

   _____

   _____

4. Is there someone who can help me practice a difficult discussion?

   _____

   _____

Gnats and Elephants

As a manager, you will have many issues to care for and a limited time in which to do this. This chapter will deal with these two items: issues and time. Since you will have multiple issues and limited time, it will be important that you take care of the most important issues as quickly as possible. Before we consider several of these issues, we must first understand the concept of Gnats and Elephants. Gnats are small, they are annoying, they usually only show up one or two at a time, and we don't usually consider them to be an issue until they are a swarm. However, gnat bites are irritating and tend to really tick people off, but we usually don't do anything about them until we are totally upset and totally frustrated. Elephants, on the other hand, are large, easily seen, and depending on the situations we find ourselves in with them, can be very scary. When we see an elephant, we get out of its way and eliminate the situation immediately. The same happens at work: you will have gnat and elephant issues with your team. As a manager you will easily see the elephant issues in your facility, office, or plant. These are major issues that everyone is aware of, and everyone communicates their concerns, and you must take care of these issues. However, the gnat's issues are often overlooked by people until they reach a level of frustration and just get ticked off to the point where they become upset and frustrated. If the gnat situations are not taken care of, people will take their frustrations out on you or others and the workplace will be disrupted, production can drop, attitudes and behaviors will change, and the high engagement of the team will suffer. To be an effective leader you must be prepared to take care of the gnats.

Gnat situations:

Parking lots that are poorly marked, full of potholes, slippery/icy, and not lighted. Just imagine how this first activity of a workday can negatively impact a person's attitude. They left home in a good mood— ready to go to work—and now they "have to deal with this."

Good leaders want to turn their employees on, not off.

Restrooms that are not clean or properly stocked with towels and toilet paper, wet slippery floors, dirty or no mirrors, and poor lighting and ventilation. One of the best leaders I have had the privilege of working with told us, "To check the health of any facility, the first place I go is to check out the condition of the restrooms. If they are not acceptable to me, then they will not be acceptable to the other employees. Why would any leader or manager think it is acceptable to treat people this way?"

Lunchrooms that are small, dirty, or inadequately equipped with refrigeration and microwaves. One of the most frustrating things employees complain about is a 30-minute lunch break: 30 or more employees competing for the 1 or 2 microwaves, dirty tables, and overflowing trash cans. These are easy fixes. Last I checked a microwave can be purchased for $150.00 or less. The convenience and extra time to enjoy a break are "priceless." Get the lunchroom crowd involved, explain the expectations of having a clean lunchroom, and ask for their ideas to improve the situation. Provide encouragement and support, but in the end it must be them that make it happen.

Loud and offensive language that can be heard by others in the lunchroom or work area. Different people get offended by different things—make sure you provide for all of the team.

Not having the proper tools or equipment to do the job effectively or efficiently. I once did some work for a manufacturing company that required their employees to keep their work area clean without slowing down production. When it was not happening, management and employees got into disagreements. After asking a few questions of the employees, it was determined that they did not mind keeping their work area clean while not disturbing production; however, to get brooms and shovels and other tools they had to walk to the maintenance area (100 feet away). The simple solution was to purchase the necessary cleaning tools and place them by each machine area and ask the employees to be responsible for the desired expectations. To no one's surprise it worked. Consider introducing 6 S and SMED workshops to the teams to help reduce waste and eliminate non-value-added activities.

There are many gnat situations that you will encounter in your career. One of the best ways to avoid the damage that can be done by these is to stay on top of the situation. Be out on the floor or office area and constantly spend time talking with your team members, listen to what they are telling you and try to see things as they do, and then if possible do something about the issue/s they bring up.

One of the most important roles of any leader is to remove the barriers which stand in the way of the team members. You may not, for certain reasons, be able to eliminate them all, but the more you remove the better the work environment becomes, and you will be viewed as an effective leader. That is a real win-win situation.

Gnats and Elephants Exercise Sheet

1. How can I arrange my daily schedule so I can have more meaningful time with my team?

    _____

    _____

2. Do I and other managers take the opportunity to eat lunch with my team in the company lunchroom? If not, what will I do to fix this situation?

    _____

    _____

3. When will I have a meeting with the rest of the management team to discuss gnats and elephants?

    _____

    _____

4. Is my location clean and safe?

    _____

    _____

Don't Ever Stop
Thinking about Tomorrow

Are you preparing you and your Business for the Future?

I encourage you to "never stop thinking about tomorrow." Unless you, your company, and your employees are fully prepared for the future, everything you have worked so hard to develop could all be lost. Believe me, tomorrow will be different and the challenges will be great. As a great leader, you have to make sure you and your team are prepared for the very fast-moving future.

A good way to prepare for the future is to begin by assessing where you are today. One way to do this is called an *internal organizational audit*, and it is different from the traditional SWOT analysis.

But before you start an internal organizational audit, several points must be emphasized. First, all involved must be totally honest in their evaluations and answers; if not, you are just blowing smoke up your own shorts and wasting time and resources. And second, use all available people in your group or organization, not just management, to get the best and most complete picture of your company's status.

Thinking about your company's **Vision and Mission** – Is the corporate vision and mission shared and understood by all? How is this done?

How often?

About your company's **Customer Base** – What is your customer base? Do you like what you see? Are your customers loyal? Will your customers allow you to make a profit? Do you know about and understand your customer's customer?

About your company's **Skills** – Do all current members of the team have the necessary skills to function in the future? Do you know what the future skill will be? What areas of training do you believe are necessary?

About your company's **Supply Chain Partnerships** – Are your suppliers competitive? How do you know? Are your inventory turns competitive? Can they be better? Are they committed to helping you get lean? What links in the chain can be removed to make your organization more competitive?

About your company's **Products or Services** – Do your products or services meet the needs of the changing world? How do your products/services compare to the competition in terms of quality, price, and delivery? How are your products/services really viewed in the marketplace? What new product/service initiatives are critical? Do you understand your customer's customer?

About your company's **Internal Communications** – What is the state of internal communications? Does the company have monthly or quarterly meetings with employees? Is there an emergency communication plan for accidents, weather emergencies, and disasters? If there is a plan, who is the spokesperson and are they prepared?

And about your company's **Cooperation** – What is the level of cooperation within your business unit? Does your unit experience what you would describe as "turf battles" or "power struggles"? How are differences resolved internally? Is everyone headed in the same direction?

Thinking about your company's **Continuous Improvement** – Do you have an ongoing Continuous Improvement or Lean Process program? Have you recently or will you in the near future look at process improvements? (Answer for both office and shop floor.) How does the company deal with "status quo"?

About your company's **Technology** – Is your company utilizing technology to its full advantage? Do you or others keep up-to-date on the kind of technology utilized in your business? Can technology help you be a better supplier to your customers?

About your company's **Ease** – Is it easy to do business with your unit or company? How would you describe the ease from the customer side? What about from the supplier side? How much "red tape" or duplication is required in the business? Are surveys and other data used to collect and analyze this information?

About your company's **Excitement** – Is there a sense of excitement in your business? What is the general feeling about your vision and values? Are people really engaged and do they say good things about the company? How well do you manage the multiple generations in the work team? What is the plan or process to help keep all focused on their future?

About your company's **Strengths** – What are the three main strengths of your unit or business? Why are they strengths? What do they do for your organization? (Really build on these.)

About your company's **Threats** – What are the three main threats to your business or your unit? Why are they threats? How could they or do they damage you?

About your company's **Competition** – How is your company viewed by your competition? What do they do that your company can't?

And about your company's **Focus** – Who does your company primarily focus on—shareholders, employees, or customers? Is the focus where it needs to be?

Once you have gathered responses from everyone in your organization, discuss them, tear them apart, and allow for open and honest input. But most of all, don't just put the results in a file somewhere—use them to develop a strategic plan. Some companies host breakfast or lunch sessions where the issues from the above list are discussed and ideas and suggestions for improvement are collected from the folks in attendance. Make sure this is not a finger-pointing or blame-game session. After all, the people that do the work really do have good ideas about how to do things more safely, faster, more profitably, and in ways that are more customer-centric. All we have to do is ask and listen.

One thing I can promise you is that tomorrow will come, and it will come whether you are ready or not. Preparing for the future is difficult work. When I started in business we used to talk about doing a 20-year plan, and we were always told the Japanese companies were doing 100-year plans. I believe that under current conditions companies should be doing 3- to 5-year planning, with a review done yearly. Customer needs and technological capabilities are changing quickly, and if you are not evaluating your company business plan annually you may suffer.

Don't Ever Stop Thinking about Tomorrow Exercise Sheet

1. How am I currently determining what tomorrow might look like?

   _____

   _____

2. How frequently do I or other managers visit with customers and have discussions about what their future needs will be?

   _____

   _____

3. How frequently do I or other managers spend time with employees to find out what they need as far as skill training or technology upgrades?

   _____

   _____

4. Who in my team would be good at facilitating an internal audit review session?

   _____

   _____

5. Does the company have tuition reimbursement available?

   _____

   _____

6. What is the overall feeling of the employees toward the company? How do I know?

   _____

   _____

Health and Living the Good Life

Often I would talk to young leaders about their work. They would always work into the fact they were working hard so tomorrow might be better for their family. They usually talked about a college education, a family vacation, a new boat or 4-wheeler so the family would have a better tomorrow. These conversations were fun to have and I enjoyed watching them accomplish these goals. We always tried to work into our discussions something about health. Every year after January 1 everyone started talking about New Year's resolutions, and many of them related to a healthier lifestyle. As a leader you must consider your personal health and how you can improve. Companies spend a lot of time and money training and developing their managers/leaders in an effort to build their bench strength and grow for the future. It has always bothered me to see companies spend all this time/effort on developing people, only to see a lot of those being developed make very bad lifestyle choices. Bad decisions on smoking, weight control, alcohol and drugs. Decisions that rob those leaders of vitality, energy, enthusiasm, and even their life. It is important to include in every management development curriculum a section on Personal Health. It is very easy in the pressure-packed life of a leader to make bad decisions on health. Training and development instructors can't make choices for people on personal matters. Having a doctor spend time with these young leaders gives them information that will allow them to make more informed choices—choices that can improve their vitality and energy and help them be better leaders. Companies spend millions on "Healthy Living" programs for their employees, but it seems like a real waste if the leaders of those people do not exhibit good habits for them to follow. The CDC has identified that productivity losses for personal and family health issues cost a company approximately $1,700.00 to $2,000.00 per year, per employee. A company leader has a responsibility to protect their organization from what many say is the single biggest financial threat to the organization—the cost of health care.

As leaders we need to make "Workplace Health" for our employees one of our major issues. To do this you, the leader, must take care of your health. Design healthy living into the fabric of the company culture by emphasizing healthy lifestyles, but most of all by "walking the talk." Set the good example—your employees are watching and a high percentage will follow your lead. Whenever possible, make sure spouses and children are involved in lifestyle discussions and activities that promote better life choices and activities. Companies I have consulted with have offered smoking cessation classes, healthy eating workshops, exercise workshops, and stress reduction seminars. If you are spending time with your teams, ask them what would be beneficial to offer. Whatever you offer and whatever the cost, the benefits will be very positive for them and the company.

Health and Living the Good Life Exercise Sheet

1. Are my lifestyle and the health decisions I make setting a positive example for the rest of the company?

   _____

   _____

2. What lifestyle change can I make to improve?

   _____

   _____

3. Do I know what health and wellness or lack of is costing this company?

   _____

   _____

4. What do health and wellness issues cost this company in terms of productivity, quality, delivery, and customer satisfaction?

   _____

   _____

Make the Investment

As a manager and leader, you will constantly strive to profitably grow your business. You will add new investors, new customers, new technology, and new equipment, and these will all take financial investments to make them happen. As you do this you must determine what rate of return you must have for each investment. Shareholders always ask, "If I give you $10.00, what will you give me in return?" You will also ask this question to those on your team that are making investments. My challenge to you is, you must consider the investment to make in your people resources. Investments in people also have rates of return, and these, in my opinion, may be the greatest and have the most lasting effect on the business. When you invest in people in the form of trust, honesty, opportunity, training, recognition, communication, caring, growth in career, expectations, follow-up/follow-through, it has been my experience that you get great returns in the form of loyal/happy, engaged employees that will drive the business to a greater level of success. All current surveys and studies show that 85–88% of employees that feel they are managed by caring individuals that recognize them and trust them will respond in like manner to that manager. Highly engaged employees are 26% more productive than their non-engaged counterparts, and the companies these engaged employees work for show 13–15% greater financial returns year over year. Invest in your people. The Gallup Organization has presented survey/study results that companies that increase their numbers of talented managers and double their rate of engaged employees achieve on average 147% higher earnings per share than their competition. Invest your time, invest finances, and invest opportunities with your most important resource—**YOUR PEOPLE**.

As Blanchard and Johnson, authors of *The One Minute Manager*, suggest: "The best minute I spend is the one I invest in people."

Make the Investment Exercise Sheet

1. Do I and the other members of the management team know what is important and of value to each of our employees? What do they consider to be an investment in them?

    _____

    _____

2. How do I/we measure the returns from this investment?

    _____

    _____

3. Is "investment in our people" part of the company strategic plan?

    _____

    _____

CPSIA information can be obtained
at www.ICGtesting.com
Printed in the USA
FSHW012210130621
82345FS

9 781478 799931